A Guide to
AMERICAN STATES

Michigan

THE WOLVERINE STATE

www.av2books.com

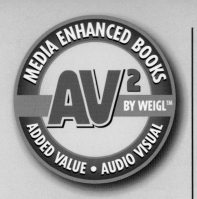

AV² provides enriched content that supplements and complements this book. Weigl's AV² books strive to create inspired learning and engage young minds in a total learning experience.

Your AV² Media Enhanced books come alive with...

Audio
Listen to sections of the book read aloud.

Key Words
Study vocabulary, and complete a matching word activity.

Video
Watch informative video clips.

Quizzes
Test your knowledge.

Go to www.av2books.com, and enter this book's unique code.

Embedded Weblinks
Gain additional information for research.

Slide Show
View images and captions, and prepare a presentation.

BOOK CODE

P 7 0 9 5 7 4

AV² by Weigl brings you media enhanced books that support active learning.

Try This!
Complete activities and hands-on experiments.

... and much, much more!

Published by AV² by Weigl
350 5th Avenue, 59th Floor
New York, NY 10118
Website: www.av2books.com   www.weigl.com

Library of Congress Cataloging-in-Publication Data

Craats, Rennay.
 Michigan / Rennay Craats.
     p. cm. -- (A guide to American states)
 Includes index.
 ISBN 978-1-61690-794-5 (hardcover : alk. paper) -- ISBN 978-1-61690-470-8 (online)
 1. Michigan--Juvenile literature. I. Title.
 F566.3.C73 2011
 977.4--dc23
                              2011018334

Printed in the United States of America in North Mankato, Minnesota

052011
WEP180511

Project Coordinator Jordan McGill
Art Director Terry Paulhus

Photo Credits
Every reasonable effort has been made to trace ownership and to obtain permission to reprint copyright material. The publishers would be pleased to have any errors or omissions brought to their attention so that they may be corrected in subsequent printings.

Weigl acknowledges Getty Images as its primary image supplier for this title.

Contents

Detroit's Renaissance Center, built in the 1970s, boasts a towering 73-story hotel, in addition to a convention center, retail stores, office space, and a theater.

Introduction

The next time you are sitting in an automobile, think of Michigan. Although Michigan is commonly known by the nickname the Wolverine State, many people also associate it with another nickname, the Auto State. Since the early 1900s, Michigan has been the location of incredible automotive breakthroughs. In 1903, the Ford Motor Company was established in Detroit. Five years later, the company produced the Model T, an automobile that was more affordable than others available at the time. Demand for the car was high. Soon, Detroit was manufacturing so many automobiles that it earned the nickname Motor City. Economic difficulties in recent years and competition from foreign car makers have led to layoffs and fewer sales for American auto

Michigan's 25,000 acres of sand dunes are a unique and fragile resource, providing ecological, recreational, and agricultural benefits.

Michigan has long been associated with the auto industry. After years of difficulties, the industry experienced a boost in 2010.

companies. Still, Michigan's auto industry, along with the entire U.S. auto industry, has bounced back. Chrysler, General Motors, and Ford continue to be among the state's major employers.

Michigan has some impressive landmarks, whether they are natural or human-made. One of them is the Renaissance Center, built in the 1970s to breathe life into Detroit's downtown core. An impressive natural site is the Sleeping Bear Dunes National Lakeshore, which stretches 35 miles along Lake Michigan's eastern coastline. It also includes North and South Manitou Islands. The park was established primarily for its outstanding natural features, including long beaches and dune formations. Tucked away on the southwest corner of South Manitou Island is a grove of white cedar trees, called the Valley of the Giants. One of the fallen trees has 528 growth rings, which means that it existed before the arrival of Christopher Columbus. Some of the trees that are still standing approach 100 feet in height.

Where Is Michigan?

Michigan is one of the Great Lakes states that make up the northern border of the United States. It is almost completely surrounded by water and is shaped like a mitten. Michigan is made up of two **peninsulas** and is almost completely surrounded by water. Many people think the Lower Peninsula is shaped like a mitten and the Upper Peninsula like a leaping rabbit.

Lake Superior forms the northern border of the Upper Peninsula. The Saint Marys River makes up the peninsula's eastern border. Lakes Huron and Michigan and the Straits of Mackinac form the southern boundary. Wisconsin serves as the western border.

The Lower Peninsula shares a border with Ohio and Indiana to the south and Lake Michigan to the west. To the north are Lakes Huron and Michigan and the Straits of Mackinac. To the east are Lake Huron, part of Ontario, Canada, and Lake Erie.

The Mackinac Bridge, nicknamed Mighty Mac, is the longest suspension bridge in the Americas. It links the Upper Peninsula and the Lower Peninsula.

There are more than 120,000 miles of paved roadways in the state. For air travelers, there are some 20 major airports throughout the state. Detroit Metro Airport, the state's busiest airport, is among the busiest in the country. In addition, there are several smaller commuter airports and airlines. Michigan is also accessible by train, with more than 3,500 miles of railroad track.

With 3,288 miles of shoreline, Michigan is bordered by more water than the entire Atlantic coastline of the United States. Only Alaska has a longer shoreline. The abundance of water in Michigan makes the state a great place for people who love water sports, such as fishing, boating, and swimming.

Lake Michigan, which forms the western border of the Lower Peninsula, is the only Great Lake that is entirely within the borders of the United States. The lake provides numerous recreational activities, such as boating and swimming.

Mapping Michigan

In many ways, bodies of water define Michigan. About 40 percent of the state's total area of 96,716 square miles is composed of the Great Lakes, and residents are never more than 85 miles from the shore of a Great Lake. The Great Lakes make up the largest freshwater surface in the world, and Lake Superior is the largest freshwater lake in the world.

Sites and Symbols

STATE SEAL
Michigan

STATE BIRD
Robin

STATE FLOWER
Apple Blossom

STATE FLAG
Michigan

STATE FISH
Brook Trout

STATE TREE
White Pine

Nickname The Wolverine State

Motto If you seek a pleasant peninsula, look about you.

Song "Michigan, My Michigan," by Douglas M. Malloch, to the tune of "Oh Tannenbaum"

Entered the Union January 26, 1837, as the 26th state

Capital Lansing

Population (2010 Census) 9,883,640 Ranked 8th state

ONTARIO

LEGEND
- Road
- River
- ★ State Capital
- • City
- Michigan
- State Border

Lake Superior

Laurium
Houghton
L Anse
Marquette
ssemer
Iron River
Manistique
Iron Mountain
Escanaba
Rhinelander
awk
Antigo
Menominee
Wausau
nfield
Stevens Point
Green Bay
De Pere
Appleton
WISCONSIN
Oshkosh
Manitowoc
Fond Du Lac
Sheboygan
Beaver Dam
Sun Prairie
Mequon
adison
Waukesha
Milwaukee
Janesville
Racine
Beloit
Kenosha
Freeport
Rockford
Waukegan
ILLINOIS
Elgin
Skokie
Dixon
Chicago
Rock Falls
Aurora
Oak Lawn

Sault Ste Marie
Sault Ste. Marie
St. Ignace
Cheboygan
Rogers City
Petoskey
Boyne City
Gaylord
Alpena
Lake Huron
Traverse City
Wurtsmith AFB
East Tawas
Cadillac
Houghton Lake
MICHIGAN
Ludington
Big Rapids
Midland
Bad Axe
Harbor Beach
Mount Pleasant
Bay City
Saginaw
Croswell
Norton Shores
Grand Haven
Grand Rapids
Owosso
Flint
Burton
Port Huron
Wyoming
Lansing
Holland
Holt
Pontiac
Troy
Farmington Hills
Detroit
Kalamazoo
Ann Arbor
Taylor
Benton Harbor
Monroe
Niles
INDIANA
South Bend
OHIO
Toledo

Lake Michigan

Lake Superior

STATE CAPITAL

Detroit served as Michigan's original territorial capital. When Michigan became a state in 1837, Detroit remained the capital. In 1847, the capital was moved to Lansing, which is more centrally located.

United States

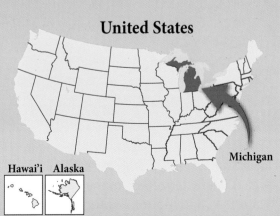

Hawai'i   Alaska

Michigan

The Land

During the last Ice Age, huge **glaciers** covered the land that is now Michigan. These glaciers shaped Michigan's two major land regions, the Central Lowland and the Superior Upland. The Central Lowland covers the eastern half of the Upper Peninsula and the entire Lower Peninsula. This region is marked by swampland, sandstone, and fertile farmland. There are sand dunes along the western section of the Lower Peninsula.

The Superior Upland covers the western half of the Upper Peninsula. This is a rough, forested **tableland** with a series of low mountain ranges, including the Huron Mountains, the Gogebic Range, and the Porcupine Range. Fast-flowing streams and waterfalls are found in this region, especially near Lake Superior. Lakes are also found in the upland region. This area is at a higher elevation than the rest of the state.

TAHQUAMENON FALLS

The Tahquamenon Falls are found near Lake Superior in the Upper Peninsula. This area is characterized by many streams, waterfalls, and mountain ranges.

SLEEPING BEAR DUNES NATIONAL LAKESHORE

The sand dunes at the Sleeping Bear Dunes National Lakeshore, along the northwest coast of the Lower Peninsula, were formed by glaciers that crushed rocks into sand.

PORCUPINE MOUNTAINS WILDERNESS STATE PARK

This state park, in the Upper Peninsula, is one of the few remaining large wilderness areas in Michigan. It has wild forests, secluded lakes, and rivers and streams.

ISLE ROYALE NATIONAL PARK

Isle Royale National Park, on an island in Lake Superior, has a rugged shoreline, clear waters, and the North Woods forest. It is accessible only by boat or plane.

Winters in Michigan can be harsh. Parts of the state
average more than 100 inches of snow each year.

Climate

S ummers in Michigan are generally warm, while winters are cold. The Great Lakes moderate the temperature somewhat, so that the weather does not usually get very hot. The Upper Peninsula is generally cooler than the Lower Peninsula. Precipitation averages 26 to 36 inches per year. Winds blowing off the Great Lakes can make for large snowfalls, called lake-effect snow. It is not uncommon to have snow piled as high as garage roofs in the Upper Peninsula.

The record high temperature in Michigan was 112° Fahrenheit at both Mio and Stanwood on July 13, 1936. The lowest recorded temperature was –51° F at Vanderbilt on Feb. 9, 1934.

Average Annual Temperatures Across Michigan

The average annual temperature varies across cities in Michigan. Why might Grosse Pointe Farms have a higher average temperature than Alberta?

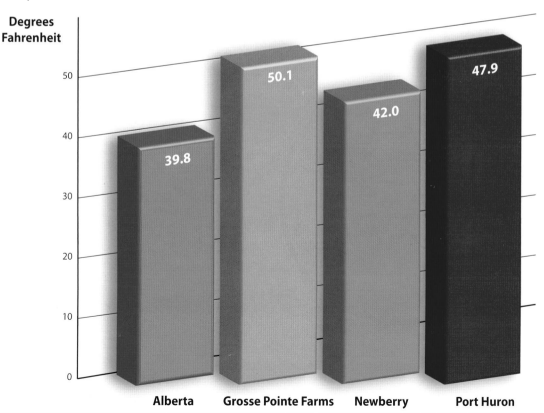

Degrees Fahrenheit

City	Degrees Fahrenheit
Alberta	39.8
Grosse Pointe Farms	50.1
Newberry	42.0
Port Huron	47.9

Natural Resources

I n the 1800s, when many parts of the United States were in the midst of a gold **boom**, Michigan was experiencing a copper boom. Copper was traditionally one of the top resources in the state. It was used for making utensils, coins, plumbing parts, and the bottoms of boats. In the late 1800s, about half of the copper in the country came from Michigan. Copper mines on Keweenaw Peninsula extended one mile into the ground. By the 1900s, larger copper deposits had been discovered in other states, and Michigan's copper deposits were being used up. Copper became less and less important to the state's economy, and Michigan's last copper mine closed in 1997.

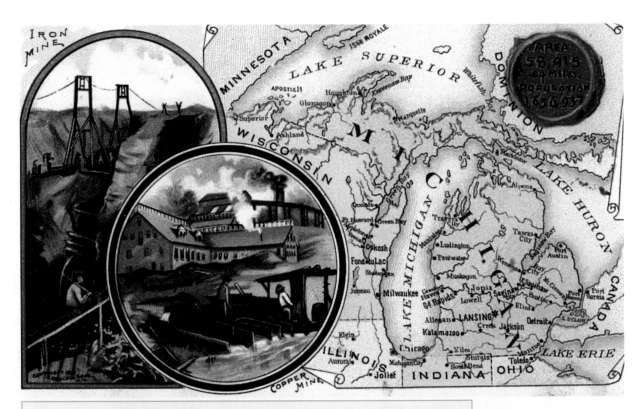

Copper and iron mining were major industries in Michigan in the 19th and 20th centuries. While copper is no longer significant, iron ore mining remains important in the state.

The salt mined in Michigan is used mainly as rock salt. It is spread on roads to reduce ice.

Today, Michigan is a leader in the production of magnesium, iron ore, gypsum, and construction sand and gravel. Limestone is also produced. The state supplies about one-fourth of the iron ore used to make steel in the United States. The ore is formed into pellets that are used to make the steel. Two large iron-ore plants in the Upper Peninsula, the Empire Mine and the Tilden Mine, produce millions of tons of pellets every year. These pellets are then shipped to major steel centers.

Limestone produced in Michigan is used to make steel and cement, as well as in buildings and landscaping projects.

I DIDN'T KNOW THAT!

The biggest limestone quarry in the world is near Rogers City in the northeast part of the Lower Peninsula.

Salt is an important resource in Michigan. Large deposits are mined near Detroit. Salt is also obtained from salt water near Midland and Saginaw.

Kalkaska sand was chosen as the state soil in 1990. Kalkaska sand is found only in Michigan. It covers about 750,000 acres in 29 counties.

Michigan's forests, land, and water are important resources that provide outdoor recreation opportunities, support 150,000 jobs, and contribute more than $12 billion each year to the state's economy.

The Michigan Natural Resources Trust Fund was set up in 1976. It provides funds to local governments and the state to buy land for public recreation or to protect land that has environmental importance or great scenic beauty.

Plants

More than half of Michigan is forested, with most of the forestland in the north. The forests consist mainly of maple, birch, oak, and spruce trees. In the 1800s, many of the state's original forests were cleared for farming. Some original forests remain, however, such as a large stand found in Hartwick Pines State Park in the Lower Peninsula. Since the early 1900s, the state has made great efforts to rebuild its forests and to protect the **endangered** trees and plants found within them. Fires, another hazard to forests, have been greatly reduced by increasing public awareness of fire regulations and by the early detection of fires.

The trillium, a flower with three delicate petals, is protected by the Michigan government. Several types of trillium flowers, including the painted trillium, are on the state's endangered list. Michiganians are not allowed to pick trilliums.

RED MAPLE

The red maple tree, one of the most abundant and widespread trees in North America, is found throughout Michigan. One of the tree's most distinctive features is its brilliant fall color.

TRILLIUM

The leaves below the trillium flower are the plant's only food source. As a result, if the flower is picked, the plant can be seriously injured and may die.

WHITE BIRCH

The white birch tree, also known as the paper birch, can grow to 70 feet high. The tree can be identified by its bright white bark, which peels easily.

APPLE BLOSSOM

The apple blossom is Michigan's state flower. The flower gives off a sweet fragrance that attracts bees, which pollinate apple trees.

The state wildflower, the dwarf lake iris, grows nowhere else in the world but in the Great Lakes region.

American chestnut trees can grow to more than 100 feet tall. The trees are valuable for animals, providing food for them to eat. Birds, deer, and squirrels all eat the nuts.

Michigan is one of the leading states in Christmas tree production.

Ferns and mosses grow in Michigan's swamp areas, as do cranberries.

Michigan flowers that bloom in the summer include the daisy, iris, orange milkweed, rose, shooting star, and tiger lily.

The white pine, which is the state tree, was chosen as a symbol of one of Michigan's greatest industries. Michigan led the United States in lumber production from 1870 to the early 1900s.

Animals

A wide range of animals live in Michigan. Animals that can be found in large numbers in parts of the state include deer, moose, bears, bobcats, and weasels. There are also some less common animals. The Kirtland's warbler is a rare North American songbird. Michiganians have been working to save this endangered **species** for decades, with some success. Until 1995, Kirtland's warblers were thought to nest only in the northern part of the Lower Peninsula. Now, though, they can be found nesting in the Upper Peninsula.

The threatened gray wolf and great antlered moose have grown in number, thanks to Isle Royale National Park in Lake Superior. Park officials have carefully studied the two species. In 1998, the wolf population had dropped to only four. There are now about 24. There are also about 850 moose on the island. Isle Royale is also home to beavers, hares, foxes, red squirrels, bald eagles, and ospreys.

AMERICAN ROBIN

The American robin, Michigan's state bird, often sings early in the morning. The male is characterized by a red breast, while the female has more muted color.

BROOK TROUT

The brook trout, the official state fish, is found primarily in northern Michigan. The fish is typically small if found in streams but can grow quite large in lakes. The state record is 9.5 pounds.

BLACK BEAR

About 90 percent of Michigan's black bears live in the Upper Peninsula. Adult males weigh up to 400 pounds.

MOOSE

The moose is native to Michigan. The male, called a bull, sheds its antlers every winter. New antlers grow in the spring.

The painted turtle is Michigan's state reptile.

Unlike many zoos, the Detroit Zoo has open animal exhibits, which give the animals a good deal of freedom to move around.

Isle Royale National Park covers 570,000 acres and includes more than 200 tiny islands in Lake Superior. It is Michigan's only national park and is dedicated to studying and preserving wildlife.

The mastodon became the state fossil in 2002. Fossils of this prehistoric mammal have been found in more than 250 places in Michigan.

More than 350 species of birds can be found in Michigan. Among them are Canada geese.

Common fish found in Michigan include whitefish, trout, salmon, walleye, and northern pike.

Tourism

Tourism is very important to Michigan's economy. About 25 million visitors spend billions of dollars in the state each year. Michigan is often associated with automobiles, but one of its tourist attractions does not even allow cars! Mackinac Island in Lake Huron offers a step back in time. With its shoreline measuring only 8.3 miles around, visitors can easily tour the island on a bicycle or horse. People can also hail a horse-drawn taxi.

The Henry Ford in Dearborn, founded by Henry Ford in 1929, is another top tourist stop. Among its attractions are the Henry Ford Museum and Greenfield Village, which includes historic buildings and aims to re-create life in America in the 1800s and early 1900s. In Dundee, there is a 225,000-square-foot retail phenomenon. Cabela's, which sells outdoor equipment and sports supplies, is no ordinary store. It has a large bronze sculpture at its entrance, a trout pond, a 40-foot mountain with a waterfall, animal displays, and a gigantic aquarium. It draws about 6 million visitors each year.

THE HENRY FORD

The museum complex known as The Henry Ford, in Dearborn, has a number of parts. One of them, Greenfield Village, includes several historic districts. Visitors can experience what life was like at different times in America's past.

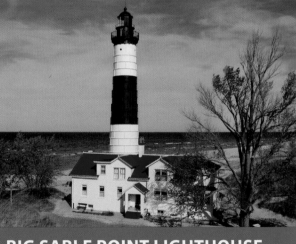

BIG SABLE POINT LIGHTHOUSE

Built in 1867 on the eastern shore of Lake Michigan, the Big Sable Point Lighthouse is open to visitors, who can explore the grounds and climb the tower. People can also live and work in the lighthouse for two-week periods.

MACKNAC ISLAND

Located in Lake Huron, Mackinac Island is a popular attraction that is a National Historic Landmark. People get around the downtown streets by walking, biking, or riding in horse-drawn carriages.

PICTURED ROCKS NATIONAL LAKESHORE

Visitors to the Pictured Rocks National Lakeshore can see beautiful beaches and sand dunes as well as sandstone cliffs and lakes. Hiking, camping, fishing, and boating are among the activities here.

I DIDN'T KNOW THAT!

The bronze sculpture outside Cabela's retail store in Dundee features two 20-foot grizzly bears. It weighs 17,000 pounds and is the largest bronze wildlife sculpture in the world.

The no-car rule applies to more than just visitors to Mackinac Island. The 500 islanders get around without cars, too. However, a small number of public utility vehicles are allowed.

The Motown Historical Museum in Detroit traces the history of the "Motown Sound." There are photographs, artwork, costumes, and other memorabilia from groups such as the Four Tops.

The Gerald R. Ford Museum in Grand Rapids includes a full-size copy of the Oval Office from when Ford was president.

Air Zoo in Kalamazoo is the leading museum of military aircraft in the United States.

Industry

Detroit has long been known as the car capital of the world. Michigan manufactures about one-quarter of the automobiles made in the country. Ford, Chrysler, and General Motors, known as the "Big Three," all established their headquarters around Detroit, and they are still there. The auto industry experienced hard times in the first decade of the 21st century, and many people in Michigan lost their jobs. Things began looking up in 2010, however.

Industries in Michigan
Value of Goods and Services in Millions of Dollars

Manufacturing makes up a significant portion of Michigan's economy. What are the most important products manufactured in Michigan?

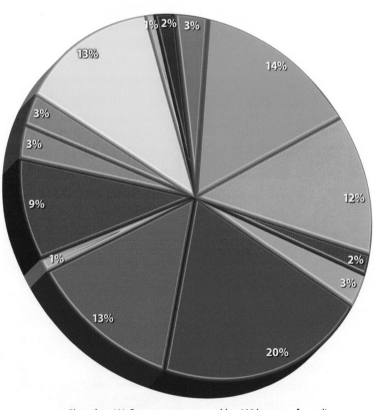

LEGEND

Agriculture, Forestry, and Fishing	$2,828
* Mining	$1,119
Utilities	$8,240
Construction	$12,171
Manufacturing	$52,953
Wholesale and Retail Trade	$45,954
Transportation	$8,618
Media and Entertainment	$12,869
Finance, Insurance, and Real Estate	$61,023
Professional and Technical Services	$74,623
Education	$2,998
Health Care	$32,246
Hotels and Restaurants	$9,318
Other Services	$9,976
Government	$46,284
TOTAL	**$368,401**

*Less than 1%. Percentages may not add to 100 because of rounding.

Chrysler has about a dozen plants in Michigan, where employees work on Chrysler, Jeep, and Dodge cars and parts.

One factor in the industry's turnaround was a new focus on producing smaller, more energy-efficient cars. In addition, the Big Three introduced new hybrid gasoline-electric cars, such as General Motors' Chevrolet Volt, and fully electric cars, such as an electric version of Ford's Focus.

The construction industry is highly dependent upon Michigan's natural resources. Limestone, a rock found along the northern coast of the Lower Peninsula, is used in steel and portland cement. Michigan's sand and gravel deposits are also mined for construction purposes. Gypsum, used to make wallboard, **lath**, and plaster, is found in the Grand Rapids area and is quarried at Alabaster.

Millions of tons of freight move through the Great Lakes each year. Both raw materials and manufactured goods are transported.

I DIDN'T KNOW THAT!

Of the top 150 automotive suppliers in North America, more than half are found in Michigan.

Well over 100,000 Michiganians work in the auto industry, and many more work in auto-related jobs.

In 1961, Ford, Chrysler, and General Motors produced 85.3 percent of the autos sold in the United States. As a result of competition from Japanese and other foreign car companies, that figure dropped to 43.5 percent in 2009.

More than 12,000 people work at agricultural jobs in Michigan.

In 2009, 18.8 percent of Michigan's workers were unionized, compared to the national average of 12.3 percent.

Some of Michigan's auto makers and other large corporations have used their research and production skills to manufacture missiles, computers, and equipment used for communication.

Goods and Services

Much of Michigan's land is farmland. There are some 55,000 farms in Michigan, and they cover 10 million acres. Fruit is very important in Michigan farming. The state is a key producer of cherries, apples, plums, strawberries, and grapes. Farmers also grow a variety of vegetables, including beans, carrots, celery, plums, asparagus, and mushrooms.

Michigan is the top producer of tart cherries in the United States. It is also one of the leaders in the production of such fruits and vegetables as apples, plums, carrots, beans, and celery.

Kellogg's products are sold in more than 180 countries around the world.

Michigan's economy relies on other kinds of manufacturing besides automobile manufacturing. Grand Rapids is known as the furniture city. The city has recently moved from low-cost to high-quality furniture production. Saginaw is a center for metal and glass manufacturing, and Muskegon is known for its billiard tables and bowling balls.

Many people start their day off with a healthy breakfast of a cereal such as Rice Krispies, Special K, or Corn Flakes thanks to Michigan's Kellogg brothers. In 1894, John and William Kellogg worked at the Battle Creek **Sanitarium**. There, they developed the first cereal flakes. In 1906, Will founded the Battle Creek Toasted Corn Flake Company. So began the cold-breakfast-cereal industry. Battle Creek is still home to the Kellogg's Company headquarters, and Kellogg's yearly sales total nearly $13 billion.

American Indians

I t is estimated that American Indians lived in the Michigan area as early as 10,000 years ago. At the time European explorers arrived in the area, Indian groups living there included the Menominee, Ottawa, Miami, Potawatomi, and Ojibwe, also called Chippewa. These groups hunted, fished, and later grew crops, such as corn, beans, and squash. They also gathered berries, herbs, and nuts. They also took advantage of the large quantities of wild rice growing in the area. The forests of the Upper Peninsula gave the Indians more than just valuable hunting grounds and a source of wood. This area was rich in copper as well. Indian groups living in the Upper Peninsula began mining copper about 5,000 years ago.

Pontiac, an Ottawa chief, was an ally of the French. He and his Indian followers joined the French in fighting the British during the French and Indian War.

Michigan's American Indians created pottery with elaborate designs. They also made sturdy birch-bark canoes, which were used for hunting and traveling. Groups traded food and goods with each other. By the 1600s, the Indians had obtained a new trading partner, the French. The Indians maintained good relations with the French. They had conflicts, however, with the British, who gained control of the area in the 1760s. Settlement of Michigan by Europeans and Americans of European heritage meant less space for the Indians. Many groups, especially the Potawatomi, were eventually forced out of Michigan and onto **reservations** in Oklahoma and Kansas.

Ojibwe women cared for the children and home. The men hunted and fished.

I DIDN'T KNOW THAT!

The Mound Builders, who were some of the earliest people living in the Michigan area, gathered piles of earth for religious and burial grounds. A ceremonial center was discovered near what is now Grand Rapids.

The Potawatomi, Ojibwea, and Ottawa shared common lifestyles and existed peacefully together.

Wild rice was so abundant in the Upper Peninsula that the Menominee did not have to grow any crops for food.

The Indians and the French respected each other when they first met and learned each other's languages.

The Indians traded the fur of beaver and other animals to the French for beads, pots, weapons, and clothing.

Explorers and Missionaries

In 1620, French explorer Étienne Brûlé became the first European to set foot in what is now Michigan. Many French fur trappers and traders flocked to the area after Brûlé's arrival. In 1679, René-Robert Cavalier, sieur de La Salle, built Fort Miami, the first French fort in the area, near present-day St. Joseph. French soldiers and farmers, led by Antoine de la Mothe, sieur de Cadillac, built Fort Pontchartrain on the Detroit River in 1701. Many other forts were soon erected, including Michilimackinac and Niles.

Antoine de la Mothe, sieur de Cadillac, founded Fort Pontchartrain in 1701 with the aid of 50 soldiers and 50 settlers. The fort developed into the city of Detroit, where Cadillac is remembered with a statue.

Missionaries who wanted to teach the Christian religion to American Indians also came to the area. In 1660, Father René Ménard arrived at the tip of the Upper Peninsula. He founded a mission at Keweenaw Bay. Father Jacques Marquette spent more than a year studying Indian languages so that he could communicate with the Indians. He established Michigan's first permanent European settlement at Sault Ste. Marie in 1668 and then traveled to Wisconsin in 1669. Upon his return to Michigan, he established another mission at St. Ignace, on the Upper Peninsula.

Timeline of Settlement

Early Exploration

1620 Etienne Brûlé becomes the first European to set foot in Michigan, reaching the St. Marys River.

1634 Jean Nicolet explores the Upper Peninsula, canoeing through the Straits of Mackinac and along the shore of Lake Michigan.

First Settlements

1660 Father René Ménard founds a mission at Keweenaw Bay.

1668 Father Jacques Marquette founds Sault Ste. Marie, the first permanent French settlement in the region.

1679 La Salle builds Fort Miami, the first French fort in the area, near present-day St. Joseph.

1701 Antoine de la Mothe, sieur de Cadillac, builds Fort Pontchartrain on the Detroit River.

Years of Conflict

1754 The French and Indian War begins, with the British, helped by some Indian groups, fighting against the French and their Indian allies.

1760 The British gain control of Michigan. The region officially comes under British control three years later, in the treaty ending the war.

1763 Pontiac, chief of the Ottawa, leads an unsuccessful rebellion against the British.

Territory and Statehood

1783 What is now Michigan becomes part of the United States at the end of the American Revolution.

1787 The U.S. Congress passes the Northwest Ordinance, establishing the Northwest Territory, which includes Michigan.

1805 The Michigan Territory is established, with Detroit as the capital.

1812–1813 During the War of 1812, Michigan is the site of battles with the British.

1837 Michigan becomes a state.

Early Settlers

O nce strongholds, such as Fort Michilimackinac on the Straits of Mackinac, were built, the next step was settling the area. Hundreds of settlers from France were eager to live in Michigan. However, after France lost the French and Indian War to Great Britain, the British took over Michigan and the fur trade.

Map of Settlements and Resources in Early Michigan

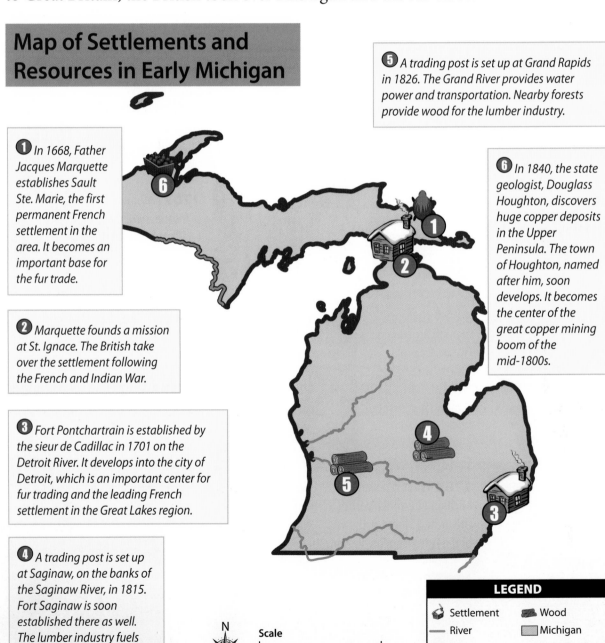

5 A trading post is set up at Grand Rapids in 1826. The Grand River provides water power and transportation. Nearby forests provide wood for the lumber industry.

1 In 1668, Father Jacques Marquette establishes Sault Ste. Marie, the first permanent French settlement in the area. It becomes an important base for the fur trade.

6 In 1840, the state geologist, Douglass Houghton, discovers huge copper deposits in the Upper Peninsula. The town of Houghton, named after him, soon develops. It becomes the center of the great copper mining boom of the mid-1800s.

2 Marquette founds a mission at St. Ignace. The British take over the settlement following the French and Indian War.

3 Fort Pontchartrain is established by the sieur de Cadillac in 1701 on the Detroit River. It develops into the city of Detroit, which is an important center for fur trading and the leading French settlement in the Great Lakes region.

4 A trading post is set up at Saginaw, on the banks of the Saginaw River, in 1815. Fort Saginaw is soon established there as well. The lumber industry fuels growth of the settlement.

N

Scale

0   100 Miles

LEGEND

🛖 Settlement		🪵 Wood	
— River		⬜ Michigan	
🦫 Fur		━ State Border	
⛏ Mining			

Rather than respecting the Indians, the British mistreated them. In the spring of 1763, an alliance of Indian groups in the region, led by the Ottawa Chief Pontiac, rebelled against the British. Pontiac led an attack on Detroit but failed to capture it. Not long after defeating this uprising, the British had to fight the American colonists in the American Revolution. When the Americans won their independence, they gained control of what is now Michigan. Finally, on January 11, 1805, President Thomas Jefferson signed an act creating the Michigan Territory, with Detroit as its capital.

In the early 1800s, many people from the eastern United States were afraid to move to Michigan. They had heard that the dunes and swamps posed health hazards. In 1825, the new Erie Canal across New York made it easier to travel to the Michigan Territory and to see what it had to offer. Settlers began to arrive in great numbers. The population rose from 31,640 in 1830 to more than 212,000 just 10 years later. In 1837, U.S. President Andrew Jackson signed the bill that made Michigan the 26th state.

Detroit grew rapidly after the development of the steamship, which linked the area with New York State. The first steam-powered ship to sail the Great Lakes arrived in Detroit in 1819.

Notable People

Many notable Michiganians contributed to the development of their state and country. A U.S. president, many politicians, and leaders in the areas of industry and science all have called Michigan home.

HENRY FORD
(1863–1947)

Henry Ford was born on a farm near Dearborn. He was fascinated by machinery and began working as a machinist in Detroit when he was 16, later becoming an engineer. In 1894, Ford built his first automobile. In 1898, he quit his job to work full-time on making autos, and in 1903, the Ford Motor Company was established. It revolutionized the industry. Ford's most successful product was the Model T, which was easy to operate and could be produced at low cost because of the **assembly line** that Ford used. Ford also introduced a plan whereby company profits were shared with workers.

CHARLES LINDBERGH
(1902–1974)

Charles Lindbergh was born in Detroit. He left the University of Wisconsin after two years to become a barnstormer, a pilot who performs stunts at fairs. Lindbergh became an international hero in 1927. That May, he made the first solo nonstop flight across the Atlantic Ocean, flying from New York to Paris in his plane, *Spirit of St. Louis*. In the next years, he flew around the United States, arousing interest in flight. When World War II began, Lindbergh spoke out against U.S. involvement. After the Japanese attack on Pearl Harbor, however, he supported war efforts and served as an adviser to the U.S. Army and Navy in the Pacific.

THOMAS E. DEWEY (1902–1971)

Thomas Dewey was born in Owosso. He became a successful prosecutor and district attorney in New York and eventually served three terms as governor there. In 1944, he ran unsuccessfully for president against Franklin Roosevelt. He ran again in 1948 but lost a close election to Harry Truman.

GERALD FORD (1913–2006)

Gerald Ford was born in Nebraska and moved to Grand Rapids when he was two. He served 25 years in the U.S. House of Representatives. In 1973, he became vice president of the United States. Then, when President Richard Nixon resigned in August 1974 because of the **Watergate scandal**, Ford became president. He helped rebuild the nation's morale, but he was defeated in the 1976 election.

COLEMAN YOUNG (1918–1997)

Coleman Young was born in Alabama. He moved to Detroit and was a Michigan state senator from 1965 to 1973, the year he was elected mayor of Detroit. The city's first African American mayor and one of the first black mayors of a major U.S. city, he retired in 1993 after five terms.

I DIDN'T KNOW THAT!

Alfred Hershey (1908–1997) was born in Owosso. A biologist, he conducted experiments in 1952 that showed that DNA is the genetic material of life. He was awarded the Nobel Prize for Medicine in 1969.

Glenn Seaborg (1912–1999) was born in Ishpeming. A chemist, he helped discover 10 elements, including plutonium and a substance that was named seaborgium in his honor. He was awarded the Nobel Prize for Chemistry in 1951.

Population

I n the 1950s and 1960s, Michigan's population grew rapidly, as the state's manufacturing industries were growing and jobs were plentiful. Population growth slowed in the late 20th century, and between 2000 and 2010, the state's population decreased by just under 1 percent. According to the results of the 2010 Census, the state population is more than 9.8 million. About 80 percent of Michiganians live in cities, and the population is most heavily concentrated in the Lower Peninsula. The state's largest city, Detroit, has more than 910,000 residents. Nearly half of the state's population lives in the Detroit **metropolitan area**. By contrast, the largest Upper Peninsula city, Marquette, has 21,000 residents.

Michigan Population 1950–2010

Michigan remains the eighth-largest state in terms of population, but the number of people living in Michigan went down between the years 2000 and 2010. Why might Michigan's population have decreased in size?

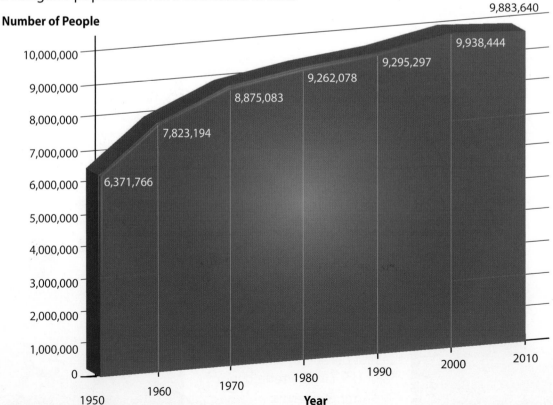

Number of People

10,000,000

9,000,000

8,000,000

7,000,000

6,000,000

5,000,000

4,000,000

3,000,000

2,000,000

1,000,000

0

6,371,766

7,823,194

8,875,083

9,262,078

9,295,297

9,938,444

9,883,640

1950   1960   1970   1980   1990   2000   2010

Year

The people in Michigan have a variety of different ethnic and cultural backgrounds. Just over 14 percent of Michiganians are African American. This is higher than the national average of about 13 percent. Slightly more than 4 percent of people in Michigan are Hispanic. Asians make up slightly more than 2 percent of the population. Native Americans make up only 0.6 percent of the population, with most of them living on one of the 11 state reservations.

Education is of great importance to the state of Michigan. It spends about $11,200 each year on every student's education. The University of Michigan, established in 1817, and Michigan State University, founded in 1855, are among the largest and most well respected public universities in the United States.

The Detroit People Mover is a fully automated light-rail system operating in the city's downtown business district. Riders can board the People Mover to get to sports arenas, exhibition centers, hotels, stores, and other sites.

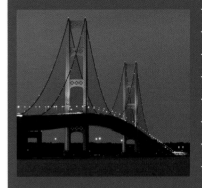

Before the Mackinac Bridge opened in 1957, people could get from the Upper Peninsula to the Lower Peninsula only by boat. The bridge connects the cities of St. Ignace in the north to Mackinaw City in the south.

Grand Rapids has the second-highest population of any city in the state, with more than 193,000 people.

Upper Peninsula residents call themselves Yoopers. This name comes from the initials of the Upper Peninsula, *UP*, pronounced "Yoo-Pee."

The University of Michigan has three campuses. They are located in Ann Arbor, Dearborn, and Flint.

Politics and Government

William Hull was Michigan's first territorial governor in 1805. At the time, Detroit was the capital. Stevens T. Mason also served as one of Michigan's territorial governors, and he became the first state governor when Michigan became a state in 1837. Since Mason was just in his 20s, he was known as the "boy governor." The state capital was moved to Lansing in 1847. The state capitol building, where the state legislature meets, was completed in 1879. It is more than a government institution. It is also very stylish. Hanging from the ceiling are 20 copper, iron, and pewter **chandeliers**. No two are alike, as they were all specially designed by Tiffany & Co. of New York. Each of these remarkable pieces weighs between 800 and 900 pounds.

The Michigan State Capitol was rededicated in 1992, following a three-year restoration project.

The dome of the State Capitol is made of cast iron and decorated with paintings done in 1866.

The state government is divided into three branches. They are the executive, the legislative, and the judicial. The executive branch, led by the governor, is responsible for making sure the laws are carried out. The governor and lieutenant governor, along with other public servants such as the secretary of state and attorney general, serve four-year terms. The legislative branch is made up of the Senate and the House of Representatives. The state's 38 senators serve four-year terms, and its 110 representatives serve two-year terms. The legislative branch creates new laws and changes existing ones. The judicial branch consists of the state's courts. Michigan's highest court is the seven-member Supreme Court.

Cultural Groups

People of many different cultures, including those of German, Polish, and Irish ancestry, call Michigan home. Many people from the Middle East also live in the state. In 1919, the first **mosque** in the United States was built in Highland Park. With more than 300,000 Arab Americans, the Detroit metropolitan area has one of the largest Arab American communities in the nation.

The African American population in Michigan is also large, especially in Detroit. About three-quarters of the city's population is African American. Many of the city's residents celebrate African American culture through events such as the African World Festival, which is held every August. More than 1 million people attend this festival to enjoy African American art, food, displays, and activities. The Charles H. Wright Museum of African American History in Detroit highlights the achievements and contributions of African Americans to the state and the country. It is the largest museum of its kind in the world.

The Islamic Center of America, located in Dearborn, is the largest mosque in North America. The building opened in 2005.

The De Zwaan windmill was built in the Netherlands in 1761. In 1964, it was moved to Holland, Michigan. It is the only authentic, functioning Dutch windmill in the United States.

Some Michiganians came to the United States from the Netherlands. There is even a city, Holland, named after their country of origin. Dutch Americans celebrate their culture during the Tulip Time Festival in Holland, which features parades, fireworks, dancing, crafts, and traditional attire, such as clogs. In the city of Frankenmuth, German culture is prominent. The city's nickname, "Michigan's Little Bavaria," is fitting. Frankenmuth is the site of the annual Bavarian Festival. This event is celebrated in June with German bands, parades, and plenty of German food.

I DIDN'T KNOW THAT!

Greektown in Detroit is a neighborhood of people of Greek heritage.

Detroit's Hart Plaza hosts different festivals every weekend during the summer. Festivals include celebrations such as the Great Lakes Irish Festival, Mexican Fiesta, and Ribs and Soul Festival.

The Frankenmuth Bavarian Inn restaurant is famous for its chicken. It serves 600,000 pounds of chicken in German recipes each year.

Hancock's Finlandia University was established in 1896, when many Finnish people were coming to Michigan to work and live. Among its courses are classes in Finnish culture and language.

Frankenmuth's Glockenspiel Tower has a 35-bell **carillon** and a clock. The tower was transported to Michigan from Germany.

Arts and Entertainment

Michigan has a vibrant art community. There are many art museums and galleries found throughout the state, including the Detroit Institute of Arts, the Flint Institute of Arts, and the Kalamazoo Institute of Arts. Many writers have called Michigan home. Illustrator and children's writer Chris Van Allsburg, from Grand Rapids, has won several awards. He received the Caldecott Medal for his illustrations in such books as *Jumanji* and *The Polar Express*. Other noted Michigan writers include Edna Ferber, Ring Lardner, and poet Theodore Roethke.

Michigan has played a large role in the U.S. music scene. Detroit is home to the original Motown Records studios. Motown became one of the most successful African American–owned businesses in U.S. history. Great singers and musicians, including Diana Ross and the Supremes, Michael Jackson, and Stevie Wonder, realized phenomenal success with Motown. Stevie Wonder, born in Saginaw, recorded his first song when he was 13 years old. Since that time, he has won many Grammy Awards and has produced numerous hit songs, including "Superstition," "You Are the Sunshine of My Life," "I Just Called to Say I Love You," and "Part-Time Lover."

Stevie Wonder signed with Motown Records when he was just 11. He has had 10 number-one hits and has sold more than 100 million albums.

Actor Tim Allen, who was raised in Michigan, has been narrating the popular "Pure Michigan" television and radio advertisements for several years.

Madonna is one of the most famous Michigan-born celebrities. This singer, dancer, and actress was born in Bay City in 1958. Other musicians and singers from Michigan include Kid Rock, Iggy Pop, Smokey Robinson, and Eminem. Many other talented Hollywood entertainers hail from Michigan. Detroit native Tom Selleck starred on the 1980s television series *Magnum, P.I.* for eight seasons. He has also enjoyed a successful film career, having starred in such movies as *Three Men and a Baby* and *Mr. Baseball*. Actor Tim Allen, who was raised in Michigan, starred in the TV series *Home Improvement* for eight seasons in the 1990s. He also does the voice for Buzz Lightyear in the *Toy Story* movies. Director Francis Ford Coppola, born in Detroit, is best known for his Academy Award–winning *Godfather* movies.

I DIDN'T KNOW THAT!

A 24-foot sculpture of a horse, based on designs done by Leonardo da Vinci, stands on display at Frederik Meijer Gardens in Grand Rapids.

Detroit's Diana Ross became a music **diva** as the lead singer of the Supremes. She has also enjoyed a successful solo career.

Comedian and Detroit native Gilda Radner was one of the original *Saturday Night Live* comedians.

Radio personality Casey Kasem, born in Detroit, hosted the popular *American Top 40* countdown show for almost 40 years before retiring in 2009.

The Interlochen Arts Academy near Traverse City teaches students in grades 9–12 about music, theater, dance, and creative writing.

Sports

From swimming to skiing, there is a sport for everyone in Michigan. Organizations such as the Michigan Mountain Biking Association lead members through the state with pedal power. Running is another popular pastime, and there are many running groups in Michigan. Some train for the Crim Festival of Races in Flint. For those looking to enjoy the outdoors at a slower pace, golf is the perfect sport, and Michigan has many world-championship golf courses. In winter, sporty Michiganians can tackle the slopes or trails at one of the state's wonderful ski resorts.

Michigan's many lakes provide numerous opportunities for people to enjoy such sports as kayaking.

There are many professional sports teams to keep Michiganians cheering. The Detroit Tigers have been have been playing major league baseball since 1901. Over the years, the Tigers have won four World Series championships. In football, the Detroit Lions battled their way to the National Football League championships four times. The Detroit Pistons of the National Basketball Association, or NBA, draw huge crowds. The Pistons won the NBA championship in 1989, 1990, and 2004. In hockey, the Detroit Red Wings have amazed fans since 1926. The team has won the Stanley Cup 11 times, most recently in 2004. The Red Wings' captain, Nicklas Lidstrom, has spent his entire career with the team, beginning in 1987.

Nicklas Lidstrom was born in Sweden. He is considered one of the best defensemen in the National Hockey League.

I DIDN'T KNOW THAT!

The Porcupine and Huron mountains receive large amounts of snow during the winter months. This makes for fantastic skiing and snowmobiling.

The U.S. Olympic Education Center at Marquette's Northern Michigan University enables athletes to train while continuing their education.

Earvin "Magic" Johnson was born in Lansing. He played college basketball at Michigan State University in the 1970s before becoming a star with the NBA's Los Angeles Lakers.

One of history's best boxers, Joe Louis, began his career in Detroit. From 1934 to 1951, Louis won 68 of 71 bouts, 54 by knockouts.

Ty Cobb, one of the best baseball players of his time, played with the Detroit Tigers from 1905 to 1926. His lifetime batting average of .367 is the highest in history.

National Averages Comparison

The United States is a federal republic, consisting of fifty states and the District of Columbia. Alaska and Hawai'i are the only non-contiguous, or non-touching, states in the nation. Today, the United States of America is the third-largest country in the world in population. The United States Census Bureau takes a census, or count of all the people, every ten years. It also regularly collects other kinds of data about the population and the economy. How does Michigan compare to the national average?

Comparison Chart

United States 2010 Census Data *	USA	Michigan
Admission to Union	NA	January 26, 1837
Land Area (in square miles)	3,537,438.44	56,803.82
Population Total	308,745,538	9,883,640
Population Density (people per square mile)	87.28	173.9
Population Percentage Change (April 1, 2000, to April 1, 2010)	9.7%	−0.6%
White Persons (percent)	72.4%	78.9%
Black Persons (percent)	12.6%	14.2%
American Indian and Alaska Native Persons (percent)	0.9%	0.6%
Asian Persons (percent)	4.8%	2.4%
Native Hawaiian and Other Pacific Islander Persons (percent)	0.2%	—
Some Other Race (percent)	6.2%	1.5%
Persons Reporting Two or More Races (percent)	2.9%	2.3%
Persons of Hispanic or Latino Origin (percent)	16.3%	4.4%
Not of Hispanic or Latino Origin (percent)	83.7%	95.6%
Median Household Income	$52,029	$48,606
Percentage of People Age 25 or Over Who Have Graduated from High School	80.4%	83.4%

*All figures are based on the 2010 United States Census, with the exception of the last two items. Percentages may not add to 100 because of rounding.

How to Improve My Community

S trong communities make strong states. Think about what features are important in your community. What do you value? Education? Health? Forests? Safety? Beautiful spaces? Government works to help citizens create ideal living conditions that are fair to all by providing services in communities. Consider what changes you could make in your community. How would they improve your state as a whole? Using this concept web as a guide, write a report that outlines the features you think are most important in your community and what improvements could be made. A strong state needs strong communities.

What features make excellent communities and states? Consider features such as education, jobs, and social services. In an ideal state, what features do you think are most essential?

In what ways does your state meet your standards for an ideal state? What services does it provide your community?

In what ways could your state be improved to bring its living conditions closer to those of an ideal state? What services should be provided in your community?

2. Your State

3. Potential Improvements

1. Ideal State

How Would You Improve Your State?

5. Solutions

4. Obstacles

What are some solutions to the obstacles that you found?

What are some obstacles that could prevent the changes you outlined from being instituted?

Exercise Your Mind!

Think about these questions and then use your research skills to find the answers and learn more fascinating facts about Michigan. A teacher, librarian, or parent may be able to help you locate the best sources to use in your research.

1 How much did Henry Ford's Model T car sell for in the early 1900s?

2 How many national flags have flown over Michigan?

3 Which city boasts the world's biggest cherry pie?

4 Which automotive firsts took place in Michigan?

5 How did the Sleeping Bear Dune get its name?

6 Who was Brigadier General George Custer?

7 What delicious drink was "accidentally" invented in Michigan?

8 Michigan has a religious claim to fame. What is it?

Words to Know

assembly line: a work arrangement in which work passes from one person or machine to the next

boom: a period of success

carillon: a set of bells, usually hanging in a tower, that are rung either mechanically or manually

chandeliers: ornamental hanging light fixtures that hold several lights

diva: a great female singer and celebrity

endangered: in danger of dying out

escarpment: a steep slope at the edge of a plateau

glaciers: large masses of slow-moving ice

lath: a thin, narrow strip of wood

metropolitan area: a large city and its surrounding communities

mosque: a Muslim temple or place of worship

peninsulas: pieces of land that are almost entirely surrounded by water

quarry: an open pit for mining resources such as stone and gravel

reservations: areas of land set aside by the government for American Indians

sanitarium: a place where people go to rest and restore their health

species: a group of animals or plants that share the same characteristics and can mate

tableland: a large region of elevated, flat land

Watergate scandal: a political scandal, involving abuse of power and obstruction of justice, that led to the resignation of President Richard Nixon in 1974

Index

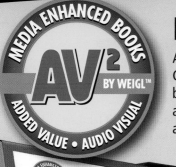

Log on to www.av2books.com

AV² by Weigl brings you media enhanced books that support active learning. Go to www.av2books.com, and enter the special code found on page 2 of this book. You will gain access to enriched and enhanced content that supplements and complements this book. Content includes video, audio, web links, quizzes, a slide show, and activities.

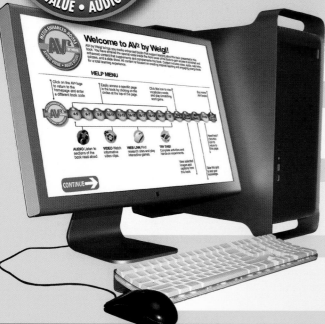

Audio
Listen to sections of
the book read aloud.

Video
Watch informative video clips.

Embedded Weblinks
Gain additional information
for research.

Try This!
Complete activities and
hands-on experiments.

WHAT'S ONLINE?

  Try This!

Test your knowledge of the state in a mapping activity.

Find out more about temperature or precipitation in your city.

Plan what attractions you would like to visit in the state.

Learn more about the early natural resources of the state.

Write a biography about a notable resident of Michigan.

Complete an educational census activity.

 Embedded Weblinks

Discover more attractions in Michigan.

Learn more about the history of the state.

Learn the full lyrics of the state song.

Video

Watch a video introduction to Michigan.

Watch a video about the features of the state.

EXTRA FEATURES

 Audio
Listen to sections of
the book read aloud.

 Key Words
Study vocabulary, and
complete a matching
word activity.

 Slide Show
View images and captions
and prepare a presentatio

 Quizzes
Test your knowledge.

AV² was built to bridge the gap between print and digital. We encourage you to tell us what you like and what you want to see in the future.

Sign up to be an AV² Ambassador at www.av2books.com/ambassador.